New Hampshire

Scenes and Seasons

New Hampshire

Scenes and Seasons

Photographs by Dick Hamilton

Text by Mark Wanner

The New England Press
Shelburne, Vermont

Designed by Andrea Gray
First Edition

ISBN 0-933050-72-0
Library of Congress Catalog Card Number: 89-60636

For additional copies or for a catalog
of our other titles, please write:

The New England Press
P.O. Box 575
Shelburne, Vermont 05482

Printed in Hong Kong
Through Four Colour Imports, Ltd,
Louisville, Kentucky.

New Hampshire
Summit to Sea
by Mark Wanner

There are only six states in the Union smaller than New Hampshire. Yet despite its small size (only 9,304 square miles), New Hampshire has a lot to offer to those who venture within its borders. A vibrant historical legacy can be found in the southern towns. A short but beautiful stretch of coastline forms the boundary to the southeast. A network of lakes dots the central part of the state, highlighted by grand Lake Winnipesaukee. And the White Mountains in the north tower above every other mountain range in the Northeast. So despite the fact that the drive from Hampton in the south to Errol in the north only takes about three hours, the journey leads past a variety of natural and cultural attractions that would take years to explore.

Despite its coastline, New Hampshire is the most mountainous state in New England, with over a third of the state perched 2,000 feet or more above sea level. Because of the diverse terrain, New Hampshire's climate is highly variable; bitter winter winds in the Presidential Range or next to the Canadian border can contrast with balmy hints of spring on the coast on the same day. The 6,288-foot summit of Mount Washington, the highest point in the east north of the Carolinas, has some of the most severe weather conditions in North America.

Most of New Hampshire's 1,027,000 current residents, as well as much of its early history, can be found in the relatively flat and mild region near the southern border. New Hampshire citizens have a history of industriousness and fierce independence, as the state motto, "Live free or die," indicates. The industrial cities of the Merrimack Valley are the traditional centers of economic and political muscle in the state. Manchester, the largest city with close to 100,000 people, and Concord, the state capital, are both located along the Merrimack River. The historic coastal region was first explored by Samuel de Champlain in 1605, and permanent settlements followed shortly thereafter. The present-day Portsmouth was New Hampshire's first center of government, but other early colonies flourished in the area and would later play roles in America's fight for independence.

The mighty Connecticut River defines the western edge of the state and forms the natural border between Vermont and New Hampshire from Canada to Massachusetts. Much of the farming in the state is done in the fertile Connecticut River Valley.

Although the south's climate and terrain are kinder to those wishing to set up households, northern New Hampshire is a wonderland for outdoor recreation. The lightly populated areas and harsh winter conditions only fuel the fervor of winter sports enthusiasts, and there are excellent facilities in the mountains for winter sports of all kinds. During the warmer months, however, a choice must be made: the same mountains will beckon for a breathtaking hike or climb, but a crystal-clear lake nearby may tempt the swimmer or fisherman, and fast-flowing rivers will attract canoeists. The prospect of sunning on a white sand beach after a bracing dip in salt water will also lead many south to the coast for at least a day . . . or maybe two. Whatever the choice, it's a no-lose situation!

History and Heritage

THE HISTORIC COAST

It wasn't long after Champlain set foot in New Hampshire that the first permanent settlements were established. Separate groups settled on the sites of what are now the cities of Dover and Portsmouth in the early 1620s, and it remains unclear which town is the state's oldest. Both lay claim to the distinction.

It's a certainty that Portsmouth became New Hampshire's first capital after incorporating as a town in 1653. An excellent harbor helped to establish Portsmouth as a vital commercial seaport, as well as a prominent shipbuilding port. The Portsmouth Naval Yard supplied ships for the War of 1812, and shipbuilding is still an important industry in the city.

The boom years of the town ended when sea transportation diminished in importance, but efforts are being made to preserve the many historical buildings and artifacts still existing from the eighteenth and nineteenth centuries. Strawbery Banke, the name of the original settlement, is now a section of the city in the middie of what used to be the seafaring community. Some thirty-five buildings from the maritime heyday have been restored, and a walk through them leads visitors back in time. Exhibits and demonstrations help to complete the illusion of being in a coastal town during a previous century. There are over thirty other buildings spread throughout the city which are open to the public and have been preserved or restored to their original splendor.

Dover was also an important shipbuilding site, but its location up the tidal Piscataqua River limited its importance as a port. Indian attacks also helped to blunt Dover's early growth. A large waterfall in the town provided the means for industrial development in later years, however, and Dover remains an important manufacturing center. Visitors to Dover can look into its history at the Woodman Institute, a collection of nineteenth-century buildings which house historical exhibits as well as natural history collections. A stroll down to Hilton's Point will show where, according to the local viewpoint, the first settlers made New Hampshire their home.

Exeter, about ten miles inland, remained uninhabited until the late 1630s, but its late start detracts little from a fascinating history, especially during the Revolutionary War. In fact, Exeter became New Hampshire's provincial capital after Portsmouth came under Tory influence during the war. It was a center of revolutionary activity, and many prominent players in the American colonists' victorious struggle established Exeter as their base. Several pre-Revolutionary War buildings have been preserved and can be seen today. Exeter's current centerpiece is Phillips Exeter Academy, a prestigious college preparatory school.

If all the museums and history lessons seem a little wearing, don't forget that the coast and some excellent beaches are only minutes away. Hampton and Rye state parks are perfect places to bake and splash cares away.

THE CITIES

New Hampshire's big cities would hardly be called "big" in most areas of the country, but they are the largest in northern New England. Concentrated in the Merrimack Valley, their economic might was built on industrial development. The textile mills that fueled urban economies in the nineteenth century have been replaced by manufacturing plants, but the cities along the Merrimack River still form the state's industrial base.

Manchester is the largest city, with a population currently pushing 100,000. The residents who named the town in 1810 were certainly correct in making the connection with one of England's industrial centers. Manchester became one of the textile centers of the world in the mid-1800s and was the location of several huge cotton mills. One of them, the Amoskeag Mills, was the largest in the world at one time. French-Canadian, Greek, and Polish workers were among those brought in to work the mills, and their descendants give Manchester a very cosmopolitan flavor today.

Manchester offers excellent resources for those interested in viewing or producing artworks. The Manchester Institute of Arts and Sciences provides continuing education in the arts and displays the works of students and local craftsmen. The New Hampshire Art Association Gallery also displays work by local artists. For those interested in art history, the Currier Gallery of Art is a nationally known museum containing American and European art. It houses an excellent collection of eighteenth- and nineteenth-century American paintings, furniture, and crafts.

Nashua and Concord are Manchester's big neighbors to the south and north. Nashua, the second largest city with about 70,000 people, is nestled next to the Massachusetts border and didn't become a part of New Hampshire until 1741. It's currently an important manufacturing center. Concord is New Hampshire's capital, and the State House is built from home-town granite. Concord supplied the granite for the Library of Congress in Washington D.C. as well. In addition to its quarrying industry, Concord has been a prominent transportation crossroads through the years. Perhaps that fact inspired the makers of the famed Concord Coach, which were instrumental in the 1800s in taming frontiers far removed from the Merrimack Valley. A Concord Coach and other artifacts of New Hampshire's past can be seen at the New Hampshire Historical Society.

New Hampshire's other cities may be smaller, but each has noteworthy features. Keene, located in the Monadnock region, possesses the widest Main Street in the world at 172 feet and has an active summer theater. Claremont, in the Connecticut River Valley, has New Hampshire's oldest Episcopal Church (1773) and Roman Catholic Church (1823). Berlin sits astride the powerful Androscoggin River in the north, and is the largest city in the area by far. Berlin's major industry is a huge paper mill, but it also serves as a winter base for skiers.

POINTS OF INTEREST

It's easy to construct a mental image of the perfect New England town. There's a quiet Main Street with the general store and post office. There's a church with a majestic steeple forming a centerpiece. Maple trees tower over a village green, making every fall glorious with a bright cascade of leaves. A small brook meanders through town, and a small bridge—maybe even a covered bridge—crosses over it on a side street.

Such towns can still be found in New Hampshire by going off the beaten track. There are many beautiful spots that don't get mentioned in books because they offer no exceptional sights or attractions. And that is part of what makes them special. A trip out to such a spot can be very rewarding, and a meditative summer picnic on the green will provide an oasis of tranquillity in a hectic day.

Other towns may have outgrown their "idyllic" stage, but they have done so gracefully and offer a visitor more to do and see. There are many special exhibits and attractions located in such small towns that are well worth searching out. Some may be worth spending a whole day seeing while others are more appropriate for a short stop; either way, any trip through New Hampshire is improved by stopping and seeing the sights in the countryside. The following are highlights of what can be seen, but the list could go on and on.

The Shaker Village in Canterbury is a collection of buildings from a Shaker community organized in 1792. The Shakers, a religious sect who fled persecution in England to settle in the new country, were noted for agricultural efficiency and craftsmanship, as well as for a strict segregation of the sexes. A museum concerned with the now nearly extinct sect is housed in onc of the buildings.

Saint-Gaudens National Historic Site in Cornish contains the house, gardens, and studio of Augustus Saint-Gaudens, a prolific and prominent American sculptor. Saint-Gaudens lived on the estate during the last seven years of his life. Many of his works are on display there, and many others can be seen at various locations throughout the United States. The extensive garden sculpture exhibit takes a while to contemplate, but it's time well spent.

Franklin Pierce, the fourteenth president of United States, was born in Hillsboro, and the Franklin Pierce Homestead still stands there. Pierce often entertained his college friend Nathaniel Hawthorne in the house before he moved on to Washington. Pierce is perhaps most memorable as having some of the worst luck of any president in history, which compounded his considerable troubles in the White House. Daniel Webster, a Massachusetts senator who left a better political legacy behind, was born in Franklin, and a replica of his boyhood home is maintained there.

Although there are many fine colleges in New Hampshire, Durham and Hanover are the state's primary college towns. Durham is home to the University of New Hampshire, while Hanover is renowned for Dartmouth College. All the facilities associated with fine research institutions can be found in both towns.

Natural Wonders

LAKES

New Hampshire's natural beauty is centered around lakes and mountains. There are approximately 1,300 lakes and ponds sprinkled throughout the state, and it's difficult to travel very far without coming across one. Most of the major lakes are easy to get to, yet remain unspoiled and crystal clear.

The largest and most celebrated lake is Lake Winnipesaukee, located in the east-central part of the state. An irregularly shaped lake with many large islands and bays, Winnipesaukee is up to three hundred feet deep, stretches almost twenty-five miles long, and is up to ten miles wide. It is a magnet for visitors, and Wolfeboro and Laconia, the two largest towns along its banks, have been resort communities since the eighteenth century.

Indians were the original inhabitants of Winnipesaukee's shores, as the name suggests. The meaning of the word has proven even more elusive than its spelling, and there are many tall tales concerning the naming of the lake. Brave braves and Indian maidens figure prominently in many of them, and it's probable that such tales have more romantic appeal than accuracy.

Finding dry land in the vicinity of Winnipesaukee proves difficult, as there are many large lakes in the immediate area. Squam, Winnisquam, Ossipee, and Newfound lakes don't have quite the resort amenities of their bigger neighbor, but all can yield large fish or be just as fun to explore. Fall foliage renders any vista in the region positively breathtaking.

Lake Sunapee, a Pennacook Indian word meaning "rocky pond," is another popular resort area. It lacks neighboring lakes but has two mountains nearby: Mount Kearsarge and Mount Sunapee. Mount Sunapee's ski area makes this area a true winter/summer playground. Lake Sunapee is large (nine miles long and three miles wide), and its setting creates a spectacular landscape.

For those looking for the spirit of adventure, the Connecticut Lakes by the Canadian border are relatively easy to drive to, and they provide recreation near the northern limits of the United States. Fishermen can pursue salmon and lake trout in their clear depths, while others might want to dip a toe in before they dive—there is a definite difference between refreshing and frigid!

MOUNTAINS

Mentioning "White Mountains" to anyone in the northeast is likely to provoke a strong response. Story after story about great hikes or ski runs may follow. Or a dreamy-eyed recounting of fall colors too brilliant to capture adequately on film. Or maybe a shiver at the memory of bone-chilling winds on a lofty summit. Those who have been through such experiences, even if only once, don't forget them.

New Hampshire's identity rests in its mountains. It's symbolic that the Old Man of the Mountain profile is the emblem of the state. Despite the steep and unforgiving terrain, local residents have carved out paths and roads, so the mountains are now readily accessible both by car and on foot. It's thus possible to delve into the very heart of the mountains, take in their majesty, and enjoy the hundreds of thousands of acres of unspoiled wilderness all around.

Mount Washington, located in the lofty Presidential Range, is the king of them all. On a clear day it can be spied from as far away as the Atlantic Ocean. Brutal weather conditions exist at the summit in winter, with winds occasionally clocked at over two hundred miles per hour combining with bitterly cold temperatures. Nevertheless, man has tamed the mountain to the point where it's not necessary to step out of the car to reach the summit. Another option is the cog railroad, which works its way up seemingly impossibly steep grades on the way to the top. However it may be reached, the summit has views that are beyond compare on a clear day.

Surprisingly, some of the other spectacular views in the area are from the bottom looking up. There are nine sheer-sided valleys—called notches—in the White Mountains, and they can be as breathtaking as any mountaintop. It's easy to feel insignificant at the base of two 1,000-foot stone walls which climb up to form the horizons on either side. And that's what it's like when traveling along the bottom of a notch.

Perhaps the most famous notch is Franconia Notch, located on I-93. The

Old Man of the Mountain juts out from the top of a cliff above the notch, but he's not easy to spot. A parking area has been built at the best viewing angle; from a view a short distance away the Old Man might look like just another bunch of rocks. Franconia Notch also has the Flume Gorge, a perpendicular chasm created by the erosion of a lava dike. Trails and bridges make the Flume easy to walk to and see. Two other large notches which are easily reached by car are Crawford Notch on Route 302 and Pinkham Notch on Route 16.

Recreation

HIKING

New Hampshire is a hiker's dream. A well-maintained and extensive network of trails crisscrosses the White Mountains, and loops of varying degrees of difficulty can be planned by using a good guide book. Beautiful day hikes are plentiful in the south.

Perhaps the most traveled trails in southern New Hampshire are those leading to the summit of Mount Monadnock in Jaffrey. The Monadnock State Reservation has camping facilities, the Monadnock Ecocenter, which informs visitors about the ecology of the mountain, and thirty miles of trails that lead to the summit. Monadnock rises 3,165 feet from generally flat terrain, and all of the other New England states can be seen from the top on a clear day.

Mount Washington is also a magnet for hikers, and its trail network allows visitors to choose which route to the top is right for them. The Ammonoosuc Ravine Trail can be used for an "easy" climb, while more challenging trails can be found on the mountain's eastern flank. No matter what trail is taken, it's wise to expect severe conditions on the summit, even during the warmer months. Many hikers have died on Mount Washington in recent years, so always bring warm clothing and proceed cautiously.

For those who are interested in challenging hikes and climbs, a series of trails in the northern part of the Presidential Range fills the bill. Most of these trails are maintained by the Randolph Mountain Club, which began building the trail network over one hundred years ago. Difficult but not dangerous hikes to the summits of Mount Madison, Mount Adams, and Mount Jefferson can be planned on Randolph Mountain Club trails. The peaks are almost a thousand feet lower than Mount Washington but are grand nonetheless; those who make it to the top will be rewarded with scenery rivaling that of any other area in the state.

DOWNHILL SKIING

A day of downhill skiing can mean very different things to different people. Some thrill to the icy bumps, sheer drops, and high speeds that get the adrenal glands going. Others want a moderate physical and mental challenge, while still others want a low-key and healthy way to get out and enjoy the mountains. All can find the perfect run for their tastes in New Hampshire.

With so much of the state perched so high, it's not surprising that there are quite a few ski areas to choose from. Most of the bigger areas are in the northern half of the state, and offer the latest snow-making and grooming equipment to augment the normally heavy snowfall. Such areas as Loon Mountain, Waterville Valley, Cannon Mountain, Wildcat, and Mount Cranmore will challenge the best and/or craziest skiers, and offer all the amenities one could wish for during a ski vacation. For those who really want to get away from it all, Wilderness/Balsams in Dixville Notch offers some great skiing within shouting distance of Canada. People who want to stay a bit farther south can ski at Gunstock, which offers high-capacity lifts near the shores of Lake Winnipesaukee. Although these areas have a higher profile, most of the ski areas in New Hampshire are small and tend to draw more local residents than out-of-state visitors. They don't have the steep vertical drops or snow-making equipment that the larger areas do, but they are also less expensive and can provide great skiing when the weather conditions are favorable. Many are also near cities and are very easy to reach, which can be a big advantage when ice and snow make long trips unwise.

Several packages are available for those who wish to try different mountains within the same region of the state; you can obtain information about such opportunities from the regional ski associations.

CROSS-COUNTRY SKIING

Working up a sweat in the middle of a New England winter may sound like a difficult thing to do, but an uphill trek on cross-country skis will quickly reveal that it's not an impossibility. New Hampshire has many touring centers which offer groomed trails, rentals, and lessons to introduce beginners to the sport.

One of the advantages of cross-country skiing is, of course, that no set trails are necessary and no ticket need be bought. Just strap on a pair of skis, set off with a compass and/or knowledgeable guide, and enjoy the quiet winter beauty of the backwoods. Golf courses frequently become informal centers for area skiers who want to stay closer to civilization.

Touring centers offer a lot to those who aren't natural pathfinders or those who take training and racing seriously. Bretton Woods and Waterville Valley have cross-country skiing facilities in addition to their downhill areas. Other touring centers include Sunset Hill and Sagamore-Hampton, which is set near the ocean. While the exhilaration of trailblazing through untouched snow isn't found at such places, most of the trails have been laid out to take advantage of the local terrain and to reward skiers who make it up a hill with a spectacular view at the top. For those who might be looking for a nordic ski vacation, several country inns operate touring centers. Each gives its guests the opportunity to spend the night in sumptuous comfort after a day of virtuous toil.

CANOEING AND KAYAKING

A canoe trip on a nearby picturesque lake or pond is possible anywhere in New Hampshire. Those who wish to find a good river run must do a little more advance planning, but there are many opportunities for river canoeing. Whether it's a placid downstream paddle or a hair-raising, technically demanding whitewater run, New Hampshire can be a canoeist's dream. And the scenery along the riverbanks will reward those who glance right or left as they descend the river.

Spring is the time to get the best whitewater runs. Always be sure to scout any unknown rapid, particularly during high water times. The Androscoggin River at Errol is perhaps the most reliable stretch of whitewater in the state, and is very popular with both kayakers and open boat enthusiasts. The rapids are difficult enough to challenge experienced canoeists, but forgiving enough for those who are ready to challenge fast-moving water in a kayak. For those wanting to test their skills to the utmost, the Contoocook River near Henniker can provide quite a ride in the spring. Be advised that only expert canoeists should attempt to run this river. The Saco River offers a variety of flatwater and rapids as it flows through the western part of the state near North Conway. Casual paddlers and experts alike can find a satisfying stretch of the river to explore when the water is high.

Only the larger rivers are reliably canoeable in deep summer, particularly during a dry year. July and August are great months to explore the flatwater stretches along the Connecticut River, however. The scenery is fantastic, and the portages, should any be encountered, are easy and well-marked. The only things to worry about are sunburn and a reluctance to leave at the take-out. A different kind of experience can be had on the tidal Piscataqua River, where the river's flow changes direction every day. A trip on the Piscataqua is a terrific way to canoe "coastal" waters safely and, if you correctly time the change of tide, a day-long "downstream" paddle (with the tide going out) can bring you right back to the starting point when the tide comes in.

Conclusion

It would take hundreds of pages to describe all that New Hampshire has to offer. The sights, places, and activities mentioned above are highlights, but only start the list of possibilities available. So even if a trip must end long before you reach Errol or Pittsburg, it shouldn't be hard to find a reason to return and perhaps delve a little deeper into all that makes New Hampshire such a special state.

Bethlehem

Washington

Swift River (*opposite*)

Stone Arch Bridge, Antrim

North Conway

View from Mount Willard (*overleaf*)

Bristol

Echo Lake, Franconia Notch (*opposite*)

Dianne's Place

Mount Washington from Littleton

Mount Monadnock from Troy

Rocky Gorge

Woodstock

Echo Lake

Baker Memorial Library, Dartmouth College

Swift River from the Kancamagus Highway

Cannon Mountain Tram II

Colonial Home, Conway

Mount Washington from Intervale (*overleaf*)

The Flume Gorge

Beaver Pond, Kinsman Notch (*opposite*)

Mount Adams

Fall scene, Hampton

Eagle Cliff and Profile Lake, Franconia Notch

State House, Concord

Whitefield

Conway Scenic Railroad

Portsmouth

The Mills in Manchester

WHITE MOUNTAIN NATIONAL FOREST
BRIDGE CONSTRUCTED BY
TOWN OF ALBANY
1858
RENOVATED 1970
WEIGHT LIMIT 6 TONS

Albany

The Old Man of the Mountain, Franconia Notch

View from the Summit of Mount Washington (*overleaf*)

The Balsams Grand Resort, Dixville Notch

Bretton Woods

Paradise Falls, Lost River Reservation

Historic Homes, Hopkinton

Bath Village and Covered Bridge

Saco River with Mount Washington in the Background (*opposite*)

Sandwich

Mount Chocorua

Summer Fields, Jefferson

Cornish-Windsor Covered Bridge (*opposite*)

Silver Cascade, Crawford Notch

Dartmouth College, Hanover

Cannon Mountain (*overleaf*)

Flume Covered Bridge

Sunset on Alton Bay, Lake Winnipesaukee

Sunset on Mount Washington, Bretton Woods

Sugar Hill Farm (*opposite*)

Mount Washington Cog Railway

Red Eagle Pond, Conway (*opposite*)